LIMINAL LANDS
foraging the margins of human habitation

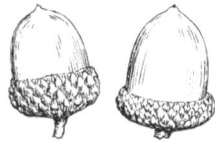

HOG PRESS

Hog Press
922 5th Street
Ames, IA 50010
USA
www.hogpress.com
editor@hogpress.com

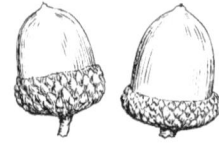

HOG PRESS

LIMINAL LANDS: FORAGING THE MARGINS OF HUMAN HABITATION.
Copyright © 2017 by Jenny Quillien and Sandra Lockwood
All rights reserved.

ISBN-13:   978-0-9848942-5-3

ISBN-10:   0-9848942-5-X

Liminal Lands
foraging the margins of human habitation

It stands to reason that writings on 'sense of place' focus on where people live. This monograph, however, respectfully turns its back on peopled environments in order to consider marginal lands—where the living ain't easy and the inhabitants few. Geography matters, indeed, limits, molds, colors human life, determines sensibilities.

Following a heuristic thread laid down by social anthropologist Victor Turner, the authors tap into the concept of liminality to scout out a path through landscape, *geographic essence*, *liminaires*, aesthetics, the sacred, *hierophantic*, back country as wellspring, *liminoids*, and our counterfeit self. The authors source two case studies in their own backyards: Lockwood's Northwest Coast of Canada and Quillien's Four Corners of the American Southwest.

Jenny Quillien
Laboratory of Anthropology
Santa Fe, New Mexico

Sandra Lockwood
Simon Fraser University
Vancouver, Canada

Coyote the Trickster.
Liminal creature par excellence in the American Southwest

Liminal Lands
foraging the margins of human habitation

". . . a place is a story, and stories are geography, and empathy is first of all an act of imagination, a storyteller's art, and then a way of traveling from here to there."

Rebecca Solnit, *The Faraway Nearby*

in the beginning was the elixir. . .

Shackleton's whiskey takes the rap for this narrative. Discovered in the abandoned Antarctic hut from the Nimrod expedition, a stash of Shackleton's booze had been repatriated to the United Kingdom and replicated. Lockwood, with her abiding fascination for explorers of the poles, had actually managed to procure a bottle. The two women took tiny sips as they visited in the cozy comfort of Lockwood's West Vancouver home while, outside, the dreary November rain pounded down on sidewalk and man.

Lockwood is a scotch drinker. Quillien is not, finds such firewater abrasive to her innards, but went for it anyway—for inspiration and for the cannibalistic experience. If one consumed Shackleton's whiskey one might acquire Shackleton's qualities: undauntable courage, physical strength, and irresistible charm.

Lockwood and Quillien had struck up a friendship when both were speakers at *Place Matters*, an AGLSP conference hosted by Stanford University. Lockwood had spoken on 'thin' places: the Arctic, the Moon, Mount Everest, those places which won't support human life but which, like magnets, continue to draw man's imagination. Quillien's talk was on 'fat' places: those *gemütlich* habitats where vernacular architecture addresses humankind's physical and psychological needs with honed aplomb.

Their respective towns, Vancouver, British Columbia, and Santa Fe, New Mexico hardly rate as hardship assignments; indeed, both are quite 'fat.' However, in both cases, when you drive out of town, you fall off the edge, so to speak. With civilization in your rear view mirror, you enter hinterlands, in-between lands, neither impossibly 'thin' like the Moon nor welcomingly 'fat' like Sussex or Virginia. These back countries have their own ineffable presence, an un-nailable *je-ne-sais-quoi*, an undeniable pull. The two friends wanted to soak up all that these marginal lands would reveal. As self-appointed 'Shackleton-lites' they had already managed a joint excursion into Quillien's American Southwest and were now headed into Lockwood's Northwest Coast.

They needed guidance and, turning to the amber liquid, asked how they were to make sense out of the jumble of their impressions and sensations.

DEFINING LIMINALITY

The muse in the bottle suggested they borrow the concept *liminality* from anthropologist Victor Turner who had borrowed it from the French folklorist Arnold Van Gennep who had revived *limen* from Latin. Etymologically, it all goes back to a threshold.

Van Gennep's interest had been in *rites de passage*: those key transformations in a lifetime when a person separates from some culturally recognized state and then re-aggregates after being 'inwardly transformed and outwardly changed.' To take a familiar example, before the marriage ceremony a person is single, throwing bachelor parties to kiss the-soon-to-be-lost condition goodbye, and afterwards the person is hitched with a different civil status and, for some, a different name. The fascinating bit is the threshold, the middle, the in-between where the person is neither single nor hitched, but moving through time, becoming.

resting in liminality

Turner's interests were forms of ritual, comparative symbology, and semiotics. He reports that he borrowed Van Gennep's concept of liminality, tossed it into his data 'like a pebble,' and began to follow the ever-spreading rings. He describes how rituals involving liminality involve symbols of *both* birth, gestation, creation, *and* death, pollution, seclusion, danger. Many African initiation rites, for example, provide a 'time-out' of separation with tests of courage and acquisition of new identities which move a boy from childhood to manhood. Such rituals might also include a symbolic striping away and grinding down of previous identities. Think of Army boot camp with loss of personal blue jeans as liminal. Frequently, the initiate hangs in a limbo of neither nor (no longer the 'before' but not yet the 'after'). Sometimes, however, the initiate hangs in a limbo of both 'this' and 'that,' androgynous, both dead and alive. In Tana Toraja, Sulawesi, babies who can't yet walk can't be classified as fully human. Should they die before their feet touch the ground they cannot be buried as a human. They will be entombed inside large trees so they might, after a fashion, continue to grow—with the tree.

Liminality, Turner points out, can be conducive to play and experimentation, where the initiate is divested of previous constraints—allowed to wander wild, play pranks—until re-aggregation is upon him and he re-enters the fold, but in a different rank. Liminality can be quick, as in a marriage ceremony, but also long, very long. Even a way of life. The anchorite and monk, just on the edge of society, are betwixt and between for the duration.

Turner went on to develop the concept of *liminoid* where various aspects of liminal situations are formalized, becoming something similar but yet different. Being an apprentice, for example, is a liminal experience (an apprentice is no longer a layman but not yet a professional); but such schooling can take on an institutional life of its own. A structured apprenticeship becomes a liminoid. Turner saw an evolutionary dynamic: today's liminal process will be tomorrow's liminoid. Yesterday, folktales like Sleeping Beauty or Little Red Riding Hood with concealed messages about maturation and sexuality were told to children around a hearth. Today, a vacation trip to Disneyland, growing up, untrustworthy wolves, good mothers, wicked step-mothers, Prince Charming: all commodified and delegated to industry.

Both Turner and Van Gennep focused on the behavioral patterns of social conundrums and their resolution. Even if the physical environment was involved—to become a man one must enter the savanna alone and kill a leopard—the physical surround was not the focus. For Quillien and Lockwood, however, it's the environment that garners the attention. Landscape is the topic. Like Turner, they gratefully borrow the concept of liminality, toss it 'like a pebble' into their own agenda—making sense of marginal country—and then follow the rings.

LIMINAL LANDS

A Londoner alights from the train in Sussex and looks around at the sweet tidy fields, the hedged lined country lanes, the orchards, and cottages. *"My my,"* she says turning to the farmer, *"you and God have certainly done a magnificent job."* *"Ah, yes,"* replies the farmer, *"and you should have seen it when God was on his own."*

First whistle stop on the sequence of rings has to be geography. It's simply obvious and commonsense that geography makes all the difference. Human history demonstrates that wide open plains facilitate movement: ask any Pole how many times they've been marched over. Mountains retard or deflect movement and to mountain regions often fall the role of buffer states: ask the never-been-conquered Bhutanese. Fertile lowlands effeminate: the children of Genghis Khan quickly eschewed their warrior habits in favor of lounging around in silk pajamas. Common morphologies of land give rise to parallel histories: beach living, be it in California, Brazil, or Australia has led to party cultures and obsession with the body beautiful. Monotheism wails outward from the monolithic and uniform desert. Elves and spirits peek out from woodlands and glens.

Encouraged by authors such as Ellen Churchill Semple, with her 1911 classic on geographic influences, and Christian Norberg-Schulz, with his work on *genius loci*, Quillien and Lockwood began speculating.

For starters, couched between 'fat' and 'thin,' liminal lands allow for human life but only on their terms. They won't yield, like Sussex, to domestication, to taming, to being reshaped in Man's image. More elemental, more aloof, they maintain a core capacity to shake off the human like a dog shakes water.

The search is for geographical indicators, not social ones. The de-militarized zone between North and South Korea, the band of weeds between the Finnish fence and the Russian fence as you take the train from Helsinki to St. Petersburg are no-man's lands and 'liminal,' but these are political constructs and of little interest here.

When does geography trump volition? That question needs to feed into definitions. And, perhaps, tight definitions aren't conducive to getting us where we want to go. Perhaps we should allow ourselves play and ambiguity:

gingerly, loosely, look at conditions and circumstances that seem to give rise to a phenomenology of liminality.

There's an attraction we need to understand: inhabitants of liminal landscapes tend to self-select; they like it there. Within the human realms of liminal living, the uncompromising unrelenting geographic limitations give rise to cultural idiosyncrasies: a sense of time that marches with more natural rhythms of earth and sky, not the wristwatch. A paucity of words: liminal soundscapes muffle and discourage trivial chattering. Standard artifacts get challenged; the land demands other truths. Bespoke local values. Emotional and physical entanglements with marginal surrounds lead to local aesthetics that accord with liminality.

GEOGRAPHIC ESSENCE

Quillien and Lockwood perceive a second ring within the general regions of their backyard hinterlands. They pinpoint smaller areas of *geographic essence* which can be characterized as follows:

Sometimes, every once in a while, the nature, aura, and spirit of a large region can get compressed into a space too small for it to plausibly hold. When this happens we can speak of *geographic essence*, a turn of phrase introduced by John Vaillant in *The Golden Spruce.*

A rather heuristic trope, isn't it? The mind scans, drone-like: Grand Canyon, La Camarge in southern France, the Straits of Magellan. People places: Jerusalem, for sure, has *geographic essence* for the Holy Lands of all religions. Perhaps Prague and Stockholm could hold their own as candidates for *geographic essence* of Old Europe. Vaillant includes Lower Manhattan on his list and suggests the cathedral of Chartres as an ecclesiastic version. Vaillant also considers greenhouses, libraries, and museums as places that can simulate the phenomenon of concentrated nature.

Such places do not derive power from being typical or average. Indeed, they will be quite specific, unique. But they will speak for a more encompassing realm. This power to evoke operates much like a good portrait of an individual conveys the psychology of that particular person but, at the same time, also informs us about humanity at large.

Vaillant leaves out vulnerability and resilience in defining *geographic essence,* but the question must be raised. Imagine Benares hit by a daily onslaught of twenty-five bus loads of camera-clicking beer-drinking tourists (say ten loads of Americans, ten of Chinese, and five German). Benares, you can bet on it, would prevail, the Holy Ganges swallowing the aliens without a blink. Other more delicate places of geographic essence–Florence comes to mind–have been brought to their knees by retailers hawking geegaws and taverns proffering watered down wine for tourists in mass transit.

So what do the Shackleton-lites find as they forage the margins of human habitation?

Northwest Coast Forests

Four Corners Rocky Plateau

Old growth forest. Vancouver Island

"This was that Earth of which we have heard,
made out of Chaos and Old Night.
Here was no man's garden, but the unhandselled globe.
It was not lawn, nor pasture, nor mead, nor woodland,
nor lea, nor arable, nor wasteland."

Henry David Thoreau, *The Maine Woods* 1864

CHAOS and OLD NIGHT
THE NORTHWEST COAST

Quillien was immediately mesmerized by the wilds of the Northwest Coast, caught in the spell of old growth forest. Forbidding. Foreboding. Eerie. Perhaps, she thought, it was akin to entering a balloon-shaped stomach, not an empty hungry one but one in full digestion. Water-logged, it smelled of dank and rot. Fetid. At best a gloomy twilight sort of light. There was no sound other than 'drip.' Moss muffled all voices and steps, and, anyway, you couldn't go anywhere. Nobody would make a mile a day in here. Phallic tree trunks drove erections toward the canopy and then collapsed limp and transgendered, joining a horizontal medley of women with moist vaginas, hips and breasts giving succor to the next generation of dicks and pricks. Without landmarks or sun and stars, all sense of direction was gone. And all sense of time. Introversion upon introversion. Worse than the most neurotic of nuclear families.

Quillien's mind wandered to 'place ballet,' a way urbanist Jane Jacobs had of describing how entrenched habits of movement and interaction gave life, direction, and meaning to healthy city sidewalks. There was place ballet here. Just not the people kind. Mites and slugs ate fallen detritus and then shit. Water dripped. Lichen and roots wormed down and took hold of detritus and shit. Water dripped. Plants sucked juices. Water dripped. Quillien thought, "This choreography can be tested: Just let me stand here a while. Pancreatic liquids would seep into my boots. Digestive mist would nibble at my eyeballs. Water would drip. I couldn't stay dry. Ineluctable death by dissolution—like an Alka Seltzer tablet."

Vaillant had described old growth forests as being "like a branched and needled Notre Dame," but had quickly added that holy and eternal won't make you comfortable. "True enough," thought Quillien, "but back out in the civilized world of British Columbia, what have we got? Vast tracks of land looking like the back side of a plucked chicken. Second growth forests that can't hold a candle to the original, and pathetic nothingnesses of tree farms scheduled from planting to harvest like a McDonald's food processing plant. Thin strip malls growing like cancerous cement kudzu vines along asphalt arteries. Tim Horton's, gas station, Stop'n'Shop, Home Depot, gas station, Starbucks. And then there was this irksome emotional tone." Quillien continued to muse: "Sentimentality and passion, like rats and mice, never inhabit the same space. Canadian twee. Shops run by sweet old ladies, lace curtains, stuffed moose-as-teddy-bear, porcelain cups and tea, greeting cards with violets and buttercups. For Christ's sake, a soporific saccharine denial of where they were. Just like the American Deep South plasters gentility lipstick over foundational aggression."

The place that John Vaillant ranked as geographic essence of this overwhelming region of endless forest of endless secrecy is an archipelago, west of west: Haida Gwaii. Roughly 4000 square miles of land, 150 to 200 islands (seems like there is no official count) with lowlands and peaks (maybe 3000 to 3500 feet but that seems guesswork as well), running 160 miles long and 70 miles wide.

The Northwest Coast poet, logger, historian, and traveler Charles Lillard concurs that Haida Gwaii is indeed a cameo of the region. Lillard kindly put together a bibliography of source material and a careful history that eschews the Wordsworthian view of Nature (human or natural) as good and kind.

Essentially, the history of Haida Gwaii reads as an opaque fog with occasional liftings of the veil for a quick glimpse about a decision to pass the place up. The veil first lifts in 1774 when explorer Juan Perez sights land but chooses to avoid a storm, dispense with claiming territory for Spain, and keep on going.

Before that, the only hint comes from a shameless, mischievous, bored Raven who wanted a place to perch and so beat his wings against the water turning the spray into rocks. That's according to the Haida whose early history is equally

Archipelago of Haida Gwaii

"Everything
is mythical
over there."
Perry Boyle,
tugboat operator
from Prince Rupert

opaque, whose language seems to be an isolate, and whose main claim to fame is the sea-faring canoe. The Haida lived not in the impossible lugubrious rain forest interior, nor on the tumultuous cold gray monster-ridden waves. They called home small scattered isolated settlements on the ribbons of beach, the liminal threshold within all the others thresholds. Fragmented fractal edges within edges.

In and out of the fog for the next 100 years are explorers and Hudson Bay Company trading ships, Floating General Stores which quickly seduced the Haida into abandoning their subsistence hunting and gathering economy in favor of securing huge quantities of pelts, allowing hunters rank that they didn't have before, and putting their class system out of kilter. Never mind. They wanted the axes, beads, knives, blankets, molasses, tobacco, liquor, and flints. The White Man motivation of Return On Investment (do any School of

Business proud they would) was well matched by native drinking, gambling, brawling, and pimping their women. The whales, fur seals, and sea otter were soon extinct and the Haida themselves came close when the 1862 smallpox epidemic killed 90% of them.

The archipelago continued to be passed up. Gold was discovered in 1851, copper in 1862, but the costs of extraction and transportation nixed operations. Logging wasn't worth it since there were easy pickings elsewhere, agriculture never attempted: the soil was poor and too wet, clearing and draining too expensive, transportation nonexistent. A personal patch for potatoes was as far as it went.

A rough estimate on population when Perez sailed on by in 1774 came in at 10,000. An 1840 guess by a certain John Work of the Hudson Bay Company puts 7000 souls on the islands. That would be just before the smallpox holocaust, which left maybe 200 to 300 people. [The extravagant Northwest Coast totem poles and potlatches made famous by anthropologists were post epidemic, desperate attempts to revive old times.] In 1917 a World War I number claims 1000 whites plus 600 Haida. Those whites weren't permanent. The war effort clamored for Sitka spruce, the best airplane wood in the world: light in weight, strong, flexible, and soft enough to take bullets without shattering. Such wood came from big trees, 500 to 800 years old. The first permanent White settler, Alexander McKenzie, came in 1887 as a Hudson Bay agent. A few years later, a certain J. L. Alexander tried to raise cattle. The cattle had no natural predators so they were happy, but with no local market and no transportation to move meat—it was just another badly hatched idea. World War II passed up Haida Gwaii: all the activity was far to the North in the Aleutians. Lillard finds a 1956 population estimate of 3000, half of which would be indigenous, then a 1967 estimate of 2200—but nobody knows how seasonal fishermen were counted. There were no internal communication links among the islands; if anybody went anywhere it was to Prince Rupert on the mainland and then back. Hippies gave it a limp attempt in the late 60s.

To inhabit a place is to be part of a place but only Raven, the Haida symbol of life's arbitrariness, and a handful of Haida inhabited. All economy was extractive and all monies made were spent elsewhere. Even Indian artifacts were extracted. Collectors as early as 1890 started amassing Haida crafts. A sea-faring canoe went for $150.

Being passed up turns out to be today's saving grace. Significant tracks of land have been declared wilderness areas, much with virgin cover—leaving Haida Gwaii with the world record for bio-mass per square acre[1]. The Southern Moresby Wilderness has more protected coastline than all the other British Columbia parks combined. Sea otters have made a comeback. 1969 marked the first 'new' totem pole and potlatch. Cultures, to remain vibrant, must tolerate some creative deviancy. Haida artists are now illustrating comic books.

The place may have more lives up its sleeve than a cat.

Cedar Mesa on the Colorado Plateau

"A land of ineffable light and sudden shadow."
Adolph Bandelier
19th century explorer

LANDSCAPE OF OBLIVION
THE COLORADO PLATEAU

The Four Corners area in the American Southwest basically means (beside the point where four states meet) the 150,000 square mile Colorado Plateau ranging in altitude from six to twelve thousand feet. It's dry, dry, dry and riddled with mountains, isolated mesa monoliths, canyons, and gulches. One of its most ardent students, wanderer Craig Childs, called it "a landscape of oblivion."

The Anasazi (a name now considered politically incorrect but everyone continues to use it) were the original peoples here. "Aborigines," Ellen Churchill Semple tells us, are "merely scientific tropes indicating the limit beyond which the movement of people cannot be traced in the gray light of an uncertain dawn." We can safely surmise that the Anasazi wandered in from all cardinal directions, different peoples speaking widely divergent languages. A plausible but unverifiable hypothesis is that the marginal unforgiving high altitude terrain offered sanctuary, if little else. We can also surmise, per Semple's observation,

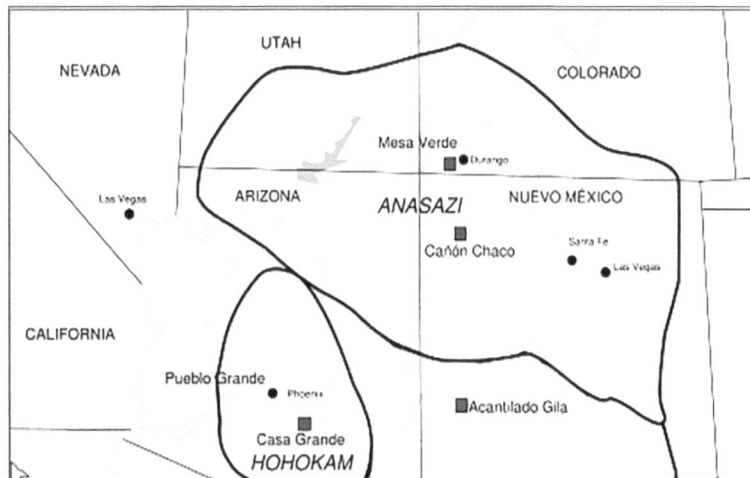

Anasazi territory

that the common morphologies of the land gave rise to parallel histories. Whatever their motley crew origins, the Anasazi faced similar problems and so developed similar technologies, architecture, and lifestyle. With the passing of centuries, they imbued the landscape with meaning and memory, further tethering themselves emotionally and spiritually to this land which, in turn, imbued them with its hubris, unified them, shut them off and shut them in.

Lockwood had been as mesmerized by the formidable presence of Southwestern landscapes as Quillien was with the presence of primeval forests. The Southwest beckons to the connoisseur of landscape with time and patience; it's not a fast read. A contented lifetime can be spent here, contemplating the architecture of geological formations, hogbacks, volcanoes, and lava flows; the variety and originality. There is no restraint here. Geological madness really. The scene kaleidoscopes every few miles, transforms with the time of day or the relief of a rain shower.

It's a tactile sort of place with stones and tumbles of boulders that invite touch. Lockwood is rock crazy. She collected what treasures she could from the arroyos, the mesa tops, the cliffs. She annoyed both airline and husband with the weight of her return luggage. She photographed the stark solitary pillars, the hoodoos, the multicolored cliffs. "How," she queried as she fussed with her camera, "does one capture scale and dignity? I've experimented with different horizon lines in the camera view finder. Nothing quite works. And the night skies here. So moving. We don't have night skies in British Columbia. I remember reading Scott's diary and his spiritual epiphany at seeing the Aurora Australis in Antarctica—and Scott was a confirmed agnostic. I get it now. But day time or night time, how can I frame the subject matter. There aren't centers here; it's all peripheries."

But, wait. If it's all peripheries, what would serve as *geographic essence*?

Mesa Verde?

The history of the Anasazi—diverse groups wandering in, wandering around (settlements were typically abandoned after a dozen or so years), their amalgamation, their rise to the splendors of Chaco in the 11th century, thick with ceremonial kivas, engineered roads, commanding Great Houses, their rapid demise, brutal fragmentation, and dispersal back into smaller, simpler, but sustainable communities—could and should serve as a vivid lesson to moderns. They ate themselves out of house and home, exploited and abused the resources, paid the piper dearly, and grew wiser.

Mesa Verde was one of the major 'fallout' settlements (12th and 13th century) after the collapse of Chaco. It does seem to qualify as geographic essence: nature, aura, and spirit of a larger region compressed into a space too small for it to plausibly hold. A stunning and achingly beautiful mesa with dwellings and kivas, hopes, dreams, and fears, clinging like swallows' nests to the sides of ravine walls. To the sides, mind you, not on top of the mesa (although there are ruins there) and not on the valley floor, but in-between, perched precariously and self-protectedly in neither nor.

Mesa Verde. Lecture on kivas

Paper cutouts.
Anasazi Heritage Center
Hovenweep

However, the question of resilience, unavoidable and obvious, rattles the cage of anyone even remotely sensitive. Mesa Verde has succumbed to discovery and national parkification, becoming a mere backdrop to gift shop, restaurant, the absurdities of throngs of visitors and the really bad jokes told by park rangers to keep the throngs amused. The ghosts have fled their former chambers and walkways, miffed no doubt by being reduced to cardboard cutout figures in 'educational' display rooms.

For the real McCoy of geographic essence in this vast landscape, one goes small, smaller, and smaller still. To Cedar Mesa. To a precarious trickle of a water seep, a hideout where a few stones placed one on the other blend in camouflage, where no gates, front doors, or house numbers speak of welcome. No park service, no signs, no Stay On Path, no Don't Touch. Raw direct intimate contact with the past. The smell is of abject terror. A granary with a meager stash of corn, the staving off of starvation, still there after 700 years, a bit worn from time and rodents, but still there. Footholds for climbing to the hideout might be found and with them complete kinetic certitude that no woman would climb up with a toddler in tow if there were any other perceivable way to survive the night.

An unvisited hideout on Cedar Mesa
A temple to absence; absences which are present

The demise of Chaco, depletion of soil and game, overspending, the splintering and fleeing of small groups must have been horrendous, an apocalypse. David Stuart in *Anasazi America* reconstructs the tale in economic terms by devising a common currency of calories: how many calories for a day of hard labor, of march, of maintaining a pregnancy and successful birth. Archaeology reveals a story of mayhem and murder. Not that far from the unvisited ruin runs a one-hundred-mile-long deep ravine, known as Grand Gulch. In one of the ruins on one of the walls of that ravine, two mummies were found. The bodies had been cut in two, the bottom half swiveled around so that the feet pointed away from the face, and then sewn back together. A disassembly and reassembly to do what? What was that all about? Guarantee dysfunction of an enemy? A walkabout in Cedar Mesa is a walkabout on memory lane. A palpably bitter, sour, desperate descent into a nightmare sort of memory.

25

The larger area of the unvisited hideout on Cedar Mesa. The dot indicates location

Perhaps as another, significantly different and far far gentler, geographic essence we could look at the Chama River Basin—quite a bit east of the big plateau but still within Anasazi territory.

On the continuum of fat-liminal-thin, the Chama basin, taking Abiquiu as its center, certainly qualifies as chubby. Reliable water, enough bottomland for an apple tree and a patch of beans and squash. Today, with a paved road, it's an easy jaunt from the main drag of the Rio Grande Valley. Here History is not lost in the 'gray light of an uncertain dawn.' History sits on the ground for easy inspection. A scattering of unexcavated Anasazi settlements, most likely 14th century (post Chaco collapse), an old hilltop hamlet founded by early Spanish subsistence farmers. Down in the reeds along the stream the remains of a settlement founded by runaway slaves and AWOL soldiers, mostly Indian and Black. New Mexico became a state in 1912, so, before that, anyone who could make it as far as the Chama basin was essentially out of Authority's spitting distance (and it didn't really matter which Authority hawked what). The recluse painter Georgia O'Keefe opted for here, seduced by the colors of the cliffs: blood, ochre, watermelon pink, dove grey, crimson, white, black, buff, honey, and steel. Upstream and then down a precarious twenty-mile dirt track, a monastery huddles by the water. Two dozen Benedictine monks live a secluded liminal life of silence and contemplation (and beer—they grow their own hops). Across the stream and up a hill, a small retreat and mosque built by the Egyptian architect Hassam Fathy. Abiquiu has always been and still is a land of escape and sanctuary.

And then, within Abiquiu, there's Bode's. If Vaillant can point to museums and libraries as places of concentration, then surely Bode's General Store (established 1893) qualifies as geographic essence. Bode's offers supplies to the area: chicken feed, nails, snow tires, the local monks' beer, cheap wines and cheap gin, canned soups, local fruit in season, bullets, knives. Bode's hosts two gas pumps and a place to pee. Given the distance between Bode's and anywhere else, most travelers stop to pee. There is even a bumper sticker available at the cash register, *I took a whizz at Bode's.*" Bode's put in a small kitchen and serves up green chili stew and tamales. Everyone cheerfully rubs shoulders: O'Keefe aficionados, Catholics and Muslims, monks and hippies, ranchers and cross country drivers headed up to Farmington. Bode's is where rock climbers and river rafters rendezvous. Bode's IS the main theater for local place ballet: Bode's IS the downtown.

Haida Gwaii survived because it was too much trouble to rape. The Colorado Plateau has now been heavily protected and parkified, but good intentions pave the road to hell. Tourism is its own Grim Reaper. Chubby insular Abiquiu drew successfully from both fat and thin but now qualifies as a sitting duck. Realtors, the weekend getaway: liminal no more. But there's still magic out there in the outback. Sheer magic. You can feel it in your bones. Quillien and Lockwood turn to the next ring created by their pebble: those few people who call these places their own.

LIMINAIRES:
INHABITANTS OF LIMINAL LANDS

Almost everybody lives in 'fat.' A cushioned existence with reserves—if one store is closed there's another down the block. A convenience existence—check the internet for the weather and set the GPS in the car. Such technological buffering dumbs down inhabitants, leaving them unable to cope without paraphernalia and dreadfully narcissistic from all the flattery dished out by consumerism and marketing. What liminality exists is of the social career ladder kind: adult versions of the child's sidewalk game. Don't step on a crack and break your mother's back. Don't step on a line and break your father's spine.

Nobody lives in Lockwood's 'thin.' Nobody really dwells on the moon, on the top of Everest, in the middle of the Sahara, in the Antarctic. Well, there are spaceships. McMurdo Base in Antarctica is a space ship, or some sort of intensive care unit with artificial tubes going in and out. Quillien once thought about going down there, to 'be on the ice.' The only job she could qualify for was in Human Resources but it sounded like a mighty strange job. People selected to go have been medically screened for every HIV, syphilis, gonorrhea, herpes, sexually transmitted disease in the books. If you're there, you're squeaky clean and what happens in McMurdo stays in McMurdo. The HR job was to deal with the fallout of unwise one night stands. And, on top of the job description, anyone on spaceship staff had to stay in the spaceship for the duration. Walkabouts were not part of the deal. "Hmm. Maybe not," sighed Quillien.

Thin is limited to expeditions. In & Out adventures. Joseph Campbell's Hero's Journey. The hero leaves home, to seek scientific knowledge, glory, a chance at promotion in a blocked hierarchy, to get away from Mom. The hero returns, older, wiser, transformed, a bit worse for the wear and tear, but collects on the adoration and fame.

Lockwood doesn't put it all down to marvelous trekking by heroes. She sees Scott's Antarctic expedition as the classic Greek tragedy: hero with an Achilles heel, chorus, fate and destiny.[2] Scott and his men: all five of them forever frozen dead.

The eye here is on *liminaires*: those who *inhabit* the marginal in-between lands and think of these lands as home. Besides inventing the noun, it's fair to invent the verb in order to say that just as apple trees 'apple' liminal lands 'liminaire.' For sure, these lands don't 'liminaire' many offspring and they are of limited varieties. Actually just two. The first, a type we might call the 'feral' individualist and then Victor Turner indirectly suggests a second kind when he talks about communitas within communities.

Turner is not concerned with the feral, but Lockwood and Quillien are. Liminal land is the classic solution for the loner, the outcast, the loser, the wanderer, the fiercely independent, and sometimes the artist. This is not to argue that fat lands are without feral components. The homeless fellow Lockwood saw this morning at the Allsup's gas station in Vancouver is feral in the eyes of the mainstream community. In Indonesia one speaks of a 'wild pig'—meaning a guy muscled into marriage and responsibility but unable to hack it, so he disappears into the edge of the woods and lives off scraps and stolen chickens. Do not cityscapes and the YMCA provide an urban purgatory with their fair share of such 'wild pigs?'

For a curious Northwest coast example of the feral individual, consider Grant Hadwin, the protagonist from John Vaillant's *The Golden Spruce.* Hadwin quite literally trained himself in feral survival skills: sheer muscular strength, tolerance to freezing waters, hunting and gathering acumen. Embodying the *both and* paradox, Hadwin is (or was) both a ferocious logger and a savior of trees. He commands general public political attention by being a loner who defies modern logging destruction by sacrificing a rare tree, a principal emblem of the Haida aborigines whose causes he supports. And for the ultimate in liminal, nobody knows if Hadwin is literally dead or literally alive—and out there on his own in the deep forest. As a legend, he is both dead and alive as well as neither dead nor alive. As a liminal legend he is undeniably present.

Many liminaires volunteer, going toward, not fleeing from. New Mexicans speak readily of 'off-the-grid.' Life styles choices of forgoing electricity, running water, and neighbors in favor of independence, solitude, and freedom on a budget of pennies. The Navajo specialize in 'off-the-grid.' Entering the Colorado Plateau from the North sometime in the late 15th century, the Navajo habitat of choice remains constant: widely dispersed homesteads, air and sky. Quillien has a Navajo friend, a weaver, who although proficient at the commercial and urban side of her art, must return to her hogan in the middle of nowhere to re-source. "To be so still," she says, "that I feel the beat of my heart in my chest." She knows that the townies' busyness and clenched-teeth determinism to get to the next appointment, to get through the day, is nothing but a shield. A shield that keeps the outside out and the vulnerable inside cocooned from actually having to step forth into the open. A shield of cowardice really. She knows that good art, of any kind, only comes from vulnerability, the touch, the genuine intimacy of self meeting the world.

There is, among the more proficient liminaires, a quality that the poet David Whyte calls 'economy of presence.' An art of maturity and few words, of attending to surrounds while the self just gets on with doing its natural thing. Whyte offers two examples. One, an old sheep dog named Cymro with an arthritic leg and blind in one eye. But that old dog knows his sheep, the terrain, his own weaknesses, and can with an admirable 'economy of presence' place himself and his good eye with a 'just rightness' and move those sheep along better than any other dog around. The other is a champion dry stonewaller from Yorkshire [who knew that stonewallers had competitions?]. Craft and speed in wall construction depend not upon sweat and grim determination but upon an ability to quietly pay attention to the emerging patterns with the available stones. Triumph stems from going with the flow, minimum exertion, minimum chipping of rocks.

With 'economy of presence' comes spaciousness, subtlety of attention. One can, for example, more fully resonate with the different times of day, taste the moods of the seasons. No doubt, it's the very frugality of life in marginal lands, the de-bloating of 'stuff,' that favors such roominess, such 'economy of presence.' With too much 'stuff' we can't see the real contours of things or the shape of time. There's an animal sort of pleasure in bringing in fire wood, finding the thick sweater, moving with the coming night and falling temperature. A pleasure unavailable in the climate-controlled city building where windows don't open. There's a pleasure in possessing only requisite belongings. A song sung in the New Mexican outback is about one blue shirt and a pair of boots that fit just right. The refrain goes, "Stuff that's real, stuff you feel. Stuff you don't hang on the wall."

The second kind of liminaire steps gingerly forward from Victor Turner's research. We must keep in mind that Turner's subject matter is the working out of *social* conundrums through ritual. His argument runs as follows: These rituals have both structure and anti-structure. It's the anti-structure which shelters a shared experience of equality and unstructuredness. It's this shared experience that dissolves antecedent social structural ties, reforms them, creating communitas, a sort of community high. Turner then says that a transient humility is acquired during these times; and it is this humility which allows people to reach a next phase in their evolution. Think boot camp buddies, the American platoons in Vietnamese jungles, and the alumni of exclusive schools. The old boys' network from the cohort of '73 and all that.

The subject matter at hand, landscape, stretches Turner's ideas. He was arguing that liminality produces optimal conditions for the emergence of communitas among liminaires. Our question becomes: Do liminal lands, because of their inherent qualities, attract or foster communities where communitas might occur?

Arguably yes. The trekkers, rock climbers, outdoorsmen of these places experience and express a 'we-ness,' a communitas. Small religious communities, such as the Abiquiu Benedictines, quite deliberately seek out the isolation, asylum, silence, and dignity of these kinds of lands. In the Southwest, the pueblo peoples, descendants of the Anasazi, with their tight quarters and relationships, kivas, secrets, initiations, are given to dancing together in the pueblos' central plazas. They repeatedly and ritually dance-as-one to maintain communitas and necessary coherences with other forces sharing their liminal world. And, then there are the Penitentes, The Brothers of Light and the Brothers of Blood. Who are they?

In the 16th and 17th centuries trickles of Spanish settlers followed the Conquistadores up El Camino Real establishing subsistence farms along the waterways. Isolated from New Spain administration, raided by Navajo, Apache, and Utes, these new entrants to the landscape struggled to eke out an existence. Distance meant that they were essentially abandoned by their government. Not only that, the Church dumped them. They were just too few, too poor, and too scattered to warrant attention and a share of the already insufficient resources. Who would take care of their spiritual needs, last rites, confession, baptism, aid the orphan and widow?

From the late 1700s the very few remaining Franciscan monks were replaced by secular priests. An identifiable folk religion took hold. The folk religion had roots, twisted perhaps, but not unattached to Catholic origins. Here's the dotted line: Back in the fatherland, on the Iberian Peninsula, a penitential tradition closely connected with *cofradías* (religious brotherhoods) had developed in the 12th century and grown in power in 16th and 17th centuries. The core was the suffering of Christ and penance. Self-flagellation was a particularly popular form thereof. To better understand this religious base, we turn to Evelyn Underhill's 1925 treatise, *The Mystics of the Church.* [3]

> If we wish to define the peculiar character of Spanish spirituality, we shall find it perhaps in an intensely austere, practical, indeed militant, temper; an outlook on realism which leaves small space for mere religious emotionalism; a tendency, once the principles of the spiritual life have been accepted, to push them at all costs to their logical end... The elaboration of organized, public, dramatic, realistic, and severe

33

The morada at Abiquiu sits on a shelf of land overlooking the valley. Photo from 1930's

Penitentes of Abiquiu with a Death Cart. Photo from 1930's

penitential expressions substantiates this persuasion, which missionaries and Conquistadores alike carried to the new world.

The Penitentes were *cofradías* which formed in the small isolated communities of New Mexico and southern Colorado. They became the government, spiritual source, and social welfare structure of their respective villages. Their dark interpretation of Catholicism was inspired by their understanding of what the missionaries had taught them. Membership was secret, male only, initiation rites were secret, although it is known that mutilation was involved. Penance was humble, anonymous, privacy protected by black hood and cloak. Easter, the stations of the cross, death and resurrection, weighed heavily over all other events in the religious calendar.

Sometimes Penitentes met in existing chapels but often they built *moradas*– separate meeting houses. Some *moradas* were on the edge of a village, some hidden in canyons, some partly below ground. They usually built them with no windows or very high ones. Again, privacy was key. The Brotherhood, was a *liminoid* per Turner's definition. Turner speaks:

> When a group of liminoid artists constitutes itself as a coterie, it tends to generate its own admission rites, providing a liminal portal to its liminoid precinct, a portal – to throw in a monster or two – guarded by three headed dogs and flaming sword angels. . . The social engineering trick is to keep the pipeline open between the society in general and each of its communitas groups.

Not a thing of the past, although both Government and Church have returned to rule, the Penitentes still carry on in the more isolated communities. Shy, unwelcoming to gawkers, and private, they continue.

The Penitentes call for another exploratory scouting step into our topic. So far, we have been asking if the inherent qualities of liminal landscape engender communities that might, in turn, engender communitas. Beyond that question, we might also ask ourselves if we learn anything else by giving ourselves permission to feel a landscape poetically. Poetic speech can be far more phenomenologically precise than long columns of facts and figures. Such knowledge would be less cerebral and more embodied; an intuitive, perhaps psychosomatic recognition of an unarticulated but already present knowing.

Travelers will recognize that the liminal lands of the New World Penitentes are not unlike the dry rugged Castilian Plateau of Mother Spain. Can the traveler, upon reading the following poetic passage, pull from within and *know*. From Alice Corbin Henderson's (1937) *Brothers of Light*:[4]

> Meanwhile, the sun sinking at our backs had turned the cliffs across the valley into splendid cathedral shapes of rose and saffron beauty—a beauty that is touched here in this country with a sometimes terrible sense of eternity, loneliness, and futility. For all the gay laughter of youth on the hillside, the stark parable of the Crucifixion is close to the country's soul. It eats into the heart, this terror; and it is not difficult to imagine how the early Franciscans felt, as they gazed upon this terrible afternoon light on bare mesa and peak, and felt the thorns of this eternal loneliness pressing into their souls. Actual mortification of the flesh is perhaps less poignant.

If the traveler can, from within, simply *know* that *Yes, I see that* or *Yes, I feel that*, then we can put forward a case for aesthetic resonance between geography and, to use an old-fashion word, soul.

AESTHETICS OF THE LIMINAL

O'Keefe dismissed

Carr dismissed

Georgia O'Keefe and Emily Carr dismissed. Yes, true, they are the two most famous painters of these landscapes. However, there is something about their renderings which is from the outside *looking at* not emerging from within. The aboriginal art seems qualitatively different, more symbiotic, more birthed from, part and parcel of the surrounding environments. Dancing masks take a first turn on center stage, for they are germane to the artistic cultures of both the Pacific Northwest and the American Southwest.

The Northwest.

John Vaillant certainly notices the landscape-art relationship:

> The Native peoples of the Northwest Coast spent most of their lives within a hundred meters of this heavily trafficked threshold, between worlds of profound inter-dependence, between the forest, the sea, and their shared inhabitants. Living in such a liminal environment, it is hardly surprising that their artworks, dances, and stories focus so heavily on convergence and transformation.

Haida Transition Mask Closed

Haida Transition Mask Open

Transformation mask collected on Haida Gwaii in 1879. When closed, the mask represents an Eagle or Thunderbird. Open, it portrays the Moon. Human hair is attached around the face of a supernatural being. The transformation of the mask is accomplished by pulling cords attached to the hinged panels that extend to form the corona.

Even a cursory scanning of Northwest Coast masks takes us back to Turner's observation of liminal states as a window for experimentation, play, a disassembly and reassembly of parts into strange combinations, opening up possibilities for new understanding and new knowledge; a sort of innovation through bricolage.

And, within the bricolage, drawing now from the classic essay by Gregory Bateson,[5] one senses a code—not necessarily an obvious code—but a code. Bateson suggests we might grasp the 'code phenomenon' by playing the word game 'Hangman' where one player thinks of a word and the other tries to guess by suggesting letters within a certain number of guesses. To play we utilize our cultural knowledge of letter combination: the *specific* word being guessed at will follow the underlying *general* rules. If the letter 't' is played, then we propose 'h,' or 'a,' or 'i,' but not 'x,' or 'v.' Hacking a computer password would be the same. Similarly, the bartender connects the specific surface observation 'Tim is on his third martini' with a more general underlying code of alcohol induced behaviors. Or, the attentive driver connects 'temperature gauge has shot up' with a mental list of possible mechanical malfunctions.

Art is more difficult in that the pool of more general rules is murkier, unarticulated, culturally specific, unconscious. The mask maker straddles the threshold, bootstrapping from his own unconscious depths, a code for carving this way not that, or putting paint here and not there on any specific mask. The observer of the mask, in equally unarticulated ways, straddles his own conscious and unconscious realms. It is through this 'straddling' that the observer enhances his own personal psychosomatic integration of surface and depth.

Bricolage. Northwest Coast Mask

Consider this mask of the Haida *gagiid*, literally 'one carried away,' a human driven mad by the experience of capsizing and nearly drowning, traumatized, caroming between worlds in a state of violent and solitary limbo. The *gagiid* gains access to deeper wisdom (and possibly health) by seeing himself in the mask. Akin, perhaps, to shell shocked soldiers with post-traumatic stress syndrome who, once unhinged, can't quite 'come home.' Therapy includes talk—saying out loud one's thoughts and then listening to oneself.

Unlike paintings by O'Keefe and Carr, these masks don't 'depict' anything. They don't 'symbolize' anything. They ARE what they are. Their own suchness. Their own spirit, distilled like grain into alcohol. To paraphrase Robert Plant Armstrong,[6] these danced masks apprehend us, as their witnesses, scrutinize us, just as much as we, their witnesses, scrutinize them. The mask, as it dances, finds us out, and we know it. What we see, for sure, is 'an object'—a mask made of wood and paint, but it is also our intimate interior world that we see. The danced mask is 'an act ever in the process of enacting itself—an instance of incarnated experience.'

In other words, the mask acts as subject because it asserts its own being, inviting recognition. At the same time, the mask acts as an object, its witnesses informing its presence. Art and its affect: it's all liminality. Both And.

Haida *Gagiid*

Kwakiutl Fool Mask. Vancouver Island

*"My body
is the awareness
of the gaze
of the other."*
Merleau Ponty

Alaskan Coast Mask

Mudhead kachina.
Zuni Pueblo

The Southwest.

From the American Southwest, consider the masked dancers of pueblo rituals, the deer and buffalo dancers who come out of the kiva, out of the *sipapu*—the threshold to the underworld from which we all come and shall return. They ARE the deer and the buffalo. They dance, imbued with recreative powers, to maintain the coherence of the universe. On the longest winter night, they dance by the light of bonfires bringing the community through to the other side of the solstice. Once danced, the animals retreat—back into the kiva and the *sipapu*. Then they emerge again, not as ordinary men, but as transformed men.

When it comes to Anasazi art and its continuation among modern pueblos, Victor Turner is once again 'our man:'

> The liminal is integrated into the total social process, the essence representing the negative and subjunctive of that total process, its possibility rather than its actuality, its may be and might have been rather than its is was and will be. The liminal may portray the inversion and reversal of secular mundane reality and social structure. The liminal can mock the gods, serve up a parody of the sacred.

Consider the pueblo trickster clown in his stripped garment free to play pranks on the crowds in the middle of festivals and break standard hierarchies. They climb high poles and throw things at onlookers. They drag a bystander into the middle of a dance. Irreverent, they mock and embarrass. Then, on the far end of the festival, in a new incarnation, they re-integrate their day jobs, pumping gas or clerking at the casino.

Consider the mudheads of the Hopi and Zuni with the very heavy responsibility of holding the kachina spirits safe from one ritual enactment to the next. Like the trickster clowns they also make appearances to poke fun and spout lewd jokes.

Buffalo Dancer

A 1936 account by Alexander Stephen[7] of the origin myth of the *Koyemsi* (mudhead) runs as follows:

> At the *atkya* (underworld) the *Tachukti* (mudhead) wore beautiful garments. He wore the same mask he has now, but it was adorned with bright parrot feathers set in a large plume just over the brow. He wore the embroidered white cotton blanket and bright woven bandoleer, the colored girdle, and other bright colored belts, fox skin at loins, breech cloth, fine netted shirt (*poronapna*), also netted leggings and blue-green moccasins. *Okiwa, siway tsoova!* Alas! He copulated with his younger sister and the Kachina chief took all his fine apparel away and doomed him from henceforth to wear a cast off woman's gown.

Associated with incest, the mudhead mask—made of cloth, mud from beneath one's feet, and seed for filling mouth and eye protrusions—has that peculiar vacant look of inbreeding. And then one thinks of pueblo living quarters and how tight they are. And then one thinks of Turner's sentence: 'the liminal is integrated into the total social process, the essence representing the negative and subjunctive of that total process.' Incest, the ultimate taboo. An adoptee would have liminal status. A child of incest? Blows the mind, doesn't it?

Importantly, the mudhead often accompanies other kachinas in rituals. "Thus," says Louis Hieb,[8] "their presence together underscores not only the physical contrasts but also the meaningful oppositions these 'persons' represent."

Rituals of Both And.

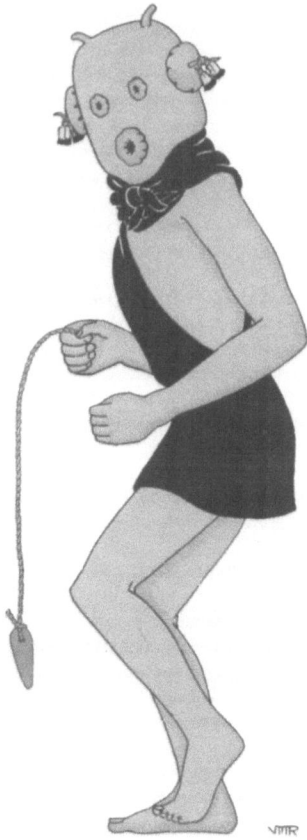

No finery for Mudheads

Mudhead Dancers. Photo possibly from 1909. Zuni Pueblo

Architecture also qualifies as an aesthetic endeavor. What do liminaires have to say about 'an aesthetic sense of place' in the way that they get themselves out of the cold Canadian rain, or the hot Southwest sun? Do the buildings, like the masks, give voice to convergence and transformation?

The immediate observation is that Pacific Northwest buildings are traditionally made of wood, which dissolves back into the earth. In the Southwest it's adobe mud brick that crumbles away. So what do we make of that?—other than it's easier and cheaper to build with what's immediately at hand.

"Life
is but a dance
around the grave."
Sigmund Freud

In New Mexico's improbable, abstract, and aloof landscape, with bony minimalist forms, time is there for the long haul. Time doesn't care much about people. Folks just come and go. There are relationships to respect here. The mountain is to the sky as the tree is to the mountain as the jay is to tree. The true children of here abide in relationship with the land knowing their place.

Mud bricks are in sync with this relationship. Adobe dwellings claim no more than temporarily molded mud; pueblos surface and sink at a tempo only somewhat slower than the jay's seasonal nest. Hogans and wood cabins are built to surrender, collapse, and depart by rot. Even the hermit's tin trailer pulled onto a ledge half way up a hill holds within the requisite temporal dis-bonding of land and inhabitant.

Destruction of liminal lands includes not just the blatant blights from logging and erosion in British Columbia or oil and gas fracking in the Four Corners. Destruction comes from the pernicious subtle undoing that accompanies people not knowing where they are. At their worst, man-made structures just don't 'get it.'

Disintegrating adobe. Near Cabezon, New Mexico

Take Tofino, the storm watcher ocean resort on Vancouver Island. Bland generic vacation rentals with mowed lawns and overpriced yuppy eateries stand obnoxiously oblivious to their incongruity with the wild and woolly coast, the sea pounding and roaring in. Geographic essence, aesthetic appropriateness, would have called for a 'sense of place,' a sense of the specific peculiarities of *this* place, the underlying pushes and pulls. It's not that the vacation rentals are atrocious; it's not the ugly which stands as the far enemy of beauty; it's the near enemy—banality and conformity.

Consider poor hapless Ojo Caliente, a hot spring just a hop, skip, and jump from Abiquiu. There was once a pueblo on the hill overlooking the spring. The ruins are there, unexcavated. Scanty records indicate that smallpox wiped out the pueblo in the 16th century. The Warm Springs Apache, as their name implies, took the spring as headquarters for rituals and rendezvous. The Hispanic settlers speckled the place with respectfully funky and ramshackle shacks which left the sacred hills alone. All these layers of man-made structures and memories simply indicated 'here.' 'Here' is geographic essence. Locals would go. Soak in the spring. Commune with place. Let their muscles and mind unwind. A time-out for regrounding. It was good.

And here come the God Damn Texan Developers with their Big Guns. Build Big. Build Permanent. Build Expensive. Build In-Your-Face. Style might be defined as composing within constraints, but the Texans saw no constraints. They bulldozed. They aped a local style deemed to have marketing appeal. Whereas true adobe and vigas had traditionally been solutions to actual building constraints, the Texans went for fake look-alikes. A commercial iconography.

With no entanglement between builder and place, no time spent together, the Texan spa buildings fail to ground themselves. Where once a mindful Hispanic villager might have placed a few ornamental tiles of blue and green, the new owners hang the list of accepted credit cards, lest the Dallas Jewish

Princess who comes to bathe think for one nanosecond that these waters were not about *her*. Might as well take a brobox into Chartres.

The springs of Ojo Caliente were once sacred and are now desecrated. Sacred cow to cash cow. But what does sacred mean anyway? And what's it got to do with liminality?

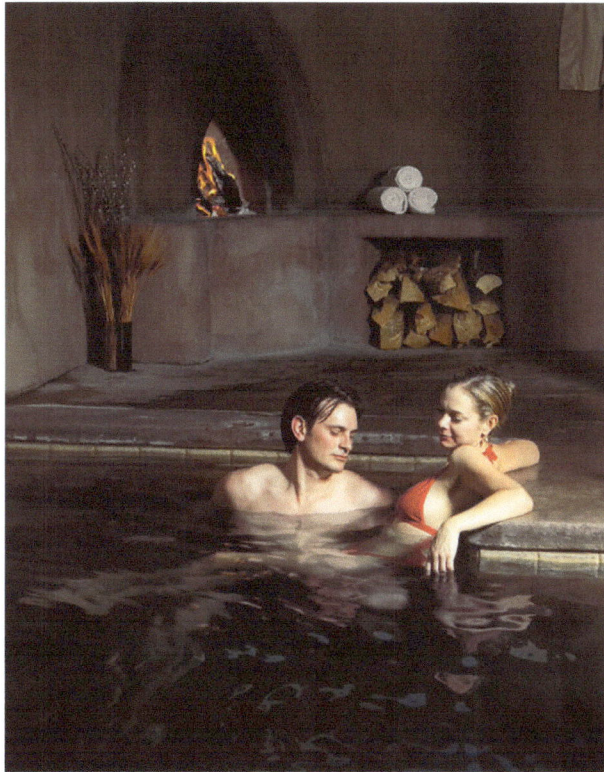

Sacred Cow to Cash Cow. Advertisement for Ojo Caliente

Lockwood makes a stab at the question and an answer.[9]

Her eye, as always, on 'thin' notices that in May of 2009 NASA astronaut Scott Parazynski can find nothing better to do than take a moon rock collected by Neil Armstrong to the summit of Mount Everest. Then, the moon rock gets twined with an Everest summit rock, and now these two have been 'churched' on an altar of an international space station, floating eternally in inter-galaxy space. What was Scott Parazynski up to?

Scott Parazynski holding up sample 10085,134 inside its protective housing

"Hierophany…" muses Lockwood, "hierophany… 'something sacred shows itself to us.' In the words of Mircea Eliade, 'by manifesting the sacred, an object becomes 'something else,' yet it continues to remain itself'…Lockwood continues to muse, "Yes, but I don't want to walk in the footsteps of the traditional, spiritual, Celtic-rocky-beach type pilgrimage place. My 'thin' heroes are more in the realm of the 20th century 'human achievement' type quest…But if I add the word 'secular' and make it 'secular hierophanies' then we're really on to something…Scott Parazynski was doing his damnedest to express liminality in the form of a secular hierophany."

There's this guy, Vaughn Hadenfeldt of Bluff, Utah who makes a modest living as guide and scout, Indiana Jones style, taking intrepid travelers into the narrow god-forsaken canyons of Ceder Mesa to experience the ruins, the hardships, and numinosity of this place. He knows of an Anasazi sandal—that's right, a sandal, an old sandal made of twisted yucca fibers, lost way back when, stuck in some crevice. He leaves it there. It's the highlight of the excursion. Just as Ayers Rock in Australia is both rock and Godhead, this old footgear is both sandal and hierophany. Hadenfeldt is a hierophant, meaning one who brings others, through pilgrimage, to the sacred.

Then there's this problem at Chaco Canyon National Park. Tourists, in the dead of night, steal out of the campsite and into the kivas with Grandma's ashes (which they brought with them in a tight container) in order to commit Grandma to the Great Beyond. Annoys the hell out of the Park Rangers. And the archaeologists too because it screws up their investigations. Whether it does Grandma any good is up for grabs. But clearly the tourist—independently of what he might want for Grandma—wants something for himself that he hasn't got in fat land.

Out having fun and getting real with the family

LIMINAL LANDS AS WELLSPRING

So, what is that tourist (aka ourselves) hankering after? As a first approximation, perhaps it is a chance to be real. Our clay bodies seeking reunion with clay Mother Earth, or some such. Some sort of Absolute, or some sort of liminal intermediary thereof, like a moon rock or a Anasazi sandal or a spring in dry land.

Thomas de Zengotita with his wicked pen, cuts us no slack about getting real about getting real. What he says is cringeworthy, but it's called for. Starting with the opening passage from his book, *Mediated.*

> Say your car breaks down in the middle of nowhere—the middle of Saskatchewan, say. You have no radio, no cell phone, nothing to read, no gear to fiddle with. You just have to wait. Pretty soon you notice how everything around you just happens to be there. And it just happens to be there in this very precise but unfamiliar way. You are *SO* not used to this. Every tuft of weed, the scattered pebbles, the lapsing fence, the cracks in the asphalt, the buzz of insects in the field, the flow of cloud against the sky, everything is very specifically exactly the way it is—and none of it is for you. Nothing here was designed to affect you. It isn't arranged so that you can experience it, you didn't plan to experience it, there isn't any screen, there isn't any display, there isn't any entrance, no brochure, nothing special to look at, no dramatic scenery or wildlife, no tour guide, no campsites, no benches, no paths, no viewing platforms with natural-historical information posed under slanted Plexiglas lectern things—whatever is there is just there, and so are you. And your options are limited. You begin to get a sense of your real place in the great scheme of things.

We are most real, points out de Zengotita, when we are at the disposal of accident and necessity. That's when we are not being addressed. That's when we go without the flattery intrinsic to representation (marketing, TV, internet, blogs, e-mail, twitter). Accident and necessity. We can't turn them off.

Back to de Zengotita. (A shortened paraphrase here.)

So, you go to Yellowstone Park for a holiday [A fine example of a liminoid is Yellowstone. An escape from the regularities of the office so as to renew with nature for a spell; but it's an institutionalized temporary escape.] You go hoping to see the wolves. They've been re-introduced and it was all over the evening news. So, you go and get lucky, and there's a bunch of cars and long lens cameras and you pull over and join the wolf watchers. Except you won't see wolves, you'll see "wolves," saying to yourself: "Wow! Cool! A Real Wolf, Not in a Cage, Not on TV. Far Out." Then, truth be told, you get restless if the "wolf" doesn't do anything. . . You start to appreciate all the editing that goes into making the Discovery Channel.

You might even start to think about *design.* How your new car is designed to isolate you from the realities of the road and the engine. How you got sucked into the flattering narcissism which underpins all automobile marketing. You were helpless out there in the middle of Saskatchewan. A true liminaire with his pickup truck would have driven with his window down listening for any abnormal clank in the motor, feeling through his own body where the wheels were in the ruts of the track. There's sanity in knowing, like the true Canadian liminaire of the plains, that the Saskatchewan boondocks doesn't give a rat's ass about you.

The persistent tourist (aka ourselves) might continue to seek out the "real," albeit in unarticulated and clumsy ways. He might self-indulgently sign up for the counterfeit "real" of Storm Chasing, Shark Diving, Bungee Jumping, A Vision Quest, Whatever. Equipped with the latest Nike tennis shoes and fashionable shades, the tourist is up for a little discomfort. A little discomfort is good. Discomfort enhances intimacy as one closes in on necessity. Hardship endows activity with authentic edge. . . making nature more "real" and therefore himself more "real." We drown in numbness without a little edge, don't we?

It's all romantic travel. Fictional. To his credit the tourist (aka ourselves) dimly perceives that his undertakings are all about separation, time-out, and plans to reaggregate. Just getting his head together, you know. But he needs to accord time, space, and place to his feelings of his head going from here to somewhere else.

"Traveling was an exploration of the deserts of my mind rather than those surrounding me.
Paul Theroux

Yeah, so, let's go light a fire in the pouring raining. But, as de Zengotita points out, it's an option. Self-appointed nature lovers experience liminal lands as contingent, fragile and contained. Contained implies packaged which implies optional. It's a choice. Options are only representation. And that means they are no more than they appear to be. And so, they are never enough.

The wolf, now "wolf," has become its own icon. Lockwood's Mt. Everest has become its own icon. McMurdo Base is MASH. Come to think of it, the replicated, handsomely packaged and handsomely sold Shackleton scotch is a simulation of itself. For de Zengotita, "Mediation crosses an ontological threshold when a thing can become its own simulation." At that point mediation transcends physical platforms of representation."

Heavy phrase: "Mediation crosses an ontological threshold when a thing can become its own simulation."

For a second approximation of 'getting real,' now imagine that the tourist (aka ourselves) could be dimly aware that the objects in his world are manipulable and manipulated representations.

Perhaps this same tourist read one of the books Craig Childs, the solo backpacker wandering the Southwest, listening, attentive to subtle patterns of rain and drought, Anasazi movements in time. Childs walked. The relationship one has with a landscape, one's understanding of it, depends on one's mode of travel. A place just isn't the same seen from a car window. Childs' wandering was subject to real accident and necessity. Childs coped. Childs knew moments of flow. Flow. The tourist, aka ourselves, would like to go there—to where flow is.

Curiously, Victor Turner made a big deal of connecting liminal communitas and flow. Flow was Turner's outermost ring in the rippling circles of inquiry after he threw the pebble of liminality into his ethnographic data.

Flow, a holistic sensation, presents itself when we act with total involvement. Where action follows action according to an internal logic, autotelic, needing no conscious intervention and providing its own reward.

So once again, the question gets stretched to landscape. Do liminal landscapes favor flow?

On the Northwest Coast, flow is undeniably germane to Vaillant's relating of British Columbian lumberjacks engaged in their craft (a sort of extreme sport matching Mihály Csíkszentmihályi's original discussion of flow). There are frames for the logger: a merging of action and awareness—but you can't become aware of being aware, or you fall off the tree. The high riggers relate the thrill of 'topping out' and fallers know their lives depend on intuitive and holistic sensing of which way a tree will go down. In the Four Corners, rock climbers speak of success as an exact and precise matching of requisite skills and demand. Each move requires a bracketing into a limited stimulus field.

Victor Turner's interest, however, wasn't in such individual experiences of flow but in a community's communitas and flow: the cessation of agonistic processes within a group and the opening up to a shared flow. Do the Penitentes experience flow as they struggle toward the next station under the weight of a heavy cross? Is their pain transfigured by the group ritual, by the collective calendar which organizes their spiritual life ? No information. Is there flow in the Benedictines' sequence of group prayer? No information.

Do liminal lands, by their nature, favor flow experiences? After all, one can make a good case for flow among addicted video gamers in fat land. How far do we want to push the analogy?

What does seem to be true is that 'the world (the real world of accident and necessity) shows up'[10] when we pay attention to unmediated objects which have a reality all their own. When we submit to the demands of a violin or irregular verbs in French or milking a cow or lighting the wretched fire in the pouring rain. When we pay attention to 'other,' outside of our own existence, then, and only then, do our real selves, not our counterfeit selves, also start to show up.

Maybe time spent in liminal landscapes, simply and in a direct uncomplicated way, favors experience and practice with the unmediated real. And, therefore, favors the development of a real self. Maybe time spent in liminal landscapes permits, like the Northwest Coast masks, a dismantling of counterfeit parts of our self and a re-assembly of real parts. And that would be the attraction.

Quillien and Lockwood sit down to review the topic of liminal landscapes with Peter Nisbet, whose paintings they chose for the cover.

Lockwood: "You paint liminal landscapes, mostly the Southwest, a bit the Pacific Coast, and you've even been to Antarctica to paint. I dare say that you paint liminality itself. The sacred, the alluring, the dangerous. And the person who contemplates your painting is standing at the threshold of the threshold."

Nisbet: "You're too kind, Miss Sandra. And you flatter the observer. A lot of times I sell a painting because the colors match the buyer's couch."

Quillien: "Come on, Pete. Don't duck the conversation."

Nisbet: "It's not easy to talk, really. I'm not a wordsmith. If I could talk it I wouldn't have to paint it, right? The Haida mask carver can't really talk either. I can't tell you what the 'code' is. I agree that a painting or a mask can be a story of sorts and that—going back to your opening quote by Solnit—a story is geography and that it's a way of travelling from here to there.

I'm not sure I want to think of myself as feral. Curmudgeon, I can't get out of that. And I cherish my time alone. And, yes, for me, liminal landscapes are a wellspring, a necessity for me to regroup. It can rattle your cage out there. The edge. Yeah. Edgy.

Geographic essence? Sure. Landscape painters are looking for it all the time. I've started working with a small drone with a camera installed so that I can find those places where it all sort of comes together. Bode's? I stop there. Gas up. Grab a bag of potato chips. Take a whizz. I wouldn't paint it.

Flow is a tough number. Economy of presence is a tough number. The two are sort of similar. There are moments when the paint just slides off my brush like butter, but mostly it's hard. Attention to what's there, the not me. Yes absolutely. I can't think too much about what I'm doing. It's a bit like your lumberjack who will fall off the tree if he starts becoming aware of being aware. Or that old chestnut about asking the centipede how he coordinates 100 legs.

Maybe what we're after is *grace*. The landscape has *grace*. Deer have *grace*. The mountain lion has *grace*. I think I've heard you quote somebody or other on the topic, Jenny. That was another conversation, a while ago. Can't remember who it was.

Quillien: Must have been Gregory Bateson[11] who was referring back to Adolf Huxley saying that *grace* was the central problem for humanity. That's a big claim—the central problem of humanity. We've lost *grace* through deceit, including self deceit. We don't know ourselves. The deer can only be themselves. Mankind is the only animal that can be not itself. Art would be one of the ways humans try to work things through. Art would be a way to find *grace*.

Nisbet: Right. We're sneaky artless bastards. You can't have *grace* if you're dishonest —or signing up for marketing flattery. It just doesn't make much sense to be dishonest when you're out on your lonesome in liminal lands. Maybe a walk on the wild side, across the Colorado Plateau or through the arctic wilderness, also counts as a search for *grace*.

As a Post Script

"We'll have just a little bit of peril, please."
Monty Python, *The Life of Brian*

These two women talking like this? Self-appointed Shackleton-lites? What a Howler! What rubbish! Rough it out there in the wilds? Ladies of the Hot-Shower-Clean-Underwear-Nice-Suppers Club these two are. They want to have their cake and eat it too.

Well, they say that they take responsibility for their cognitive dissonance. They say that there are many ways to kneel and kiss the ground. [Actually Rumi said that first.] They say their attachment to their backyard hinterlands is genuine. Quillien's heart still jumps every time a tiny piece of that intense saturated blue blue blue sky swoops down into a clearing on the back of a Rocky Mountain blue bird. Lockwood still sits in blessed silence on the porch of her Gulf Island cabin taking in the eerie half-hearted light of the Northwest.

They know they live in MeWorld, full of counterfeit everything. The top economic sector in Quillien's Santa Fe is the 'hospitality industry' selling illusions. You know, please fill out this survey about your 'experience' so that we may better serve your self-absorption.

"I am myself and my circumstances."
José Ortega y Gasset

They know they hang out at universities where the current fashion is to destabilize fixed categories and open up multiple readings in accordance with context and the needs of the moment. At its best, it is a form of play. The great Chomsky, when taking flak over his theories of language acquisition through deep structure, riposted, "Well, it was just an idea." De Zengotita calls social constructionism/deconstructionism the academic equivalent of shopping. Intellectual shopping. Hear that you academics? Just out at the mall for a stroll and a steamed-skim-milk-cinnamon-tumeric-raw-honey latte. Geography we tell you. Geography.

They know their schooling taught them to think like fat bureaucrats dependent on easy-to-read, spreadsheet-friendly, ways of accounting—uniform units such as 'square feet.' But 'square feet' don't tell you much about a place. Liminaires, such as the local herdsmen in Lesotho ask, 'how do you measure a land with feet that don't walk, don't feel the lay of the land and its texture? Irish farmers speak of land in terms of how many cows it will support. Have you got a two cow farm or a three cow farm? Old French peasants count land in the number of days it will take to plow or harvest it. Bureaucrats like simple neat maps not multi-faceted, multi-layered territories. Liminality won't be in their ken.

They know liminality is an elusive topic. Can't put it in a jar. The energy of liminality emerges from ambiguity. Any ethnography of it is, by definition, a liminal endeavor. The ethnographer has to be both inside the place of study and outside. That's the whole point.

Quillien and Lockwood know they need more time 'out there,' slow time—walking speed time, not square feet time. They know they need to practice lighting a fire in the pouring rain. Armchair anthropology won't cut muster. And they know—Yeah. Yeah.—They know the Buddha said, "You cannot travel the path before you have become the path itself."

And they know there's still some scotch in that bottle.

Raven,
the mischievous creature
of liminality on the Northwest Coast.

END NOTES

1. nationalgeographic.com/travel/canada/haida-gwaii-britsh-columbia.

2. Lockwood, Sandra. "*Scott of the Antarctic as Greek Tragedy.*" Tri-University Colloquium for Theatre and Performance Research. University of British Columbia. April 30, 2016.

3. Underhill, Evelyn. *The Mystics of the Church* (1925) page 168, quoted in Weigle's *Brothers of Light Brothers of Blood*, Chapter 1.

4. Alice Corbin Henderson. *Brothers of Light* (1937) page 35, quoted in Weigle's *Brothers of Light Brothers of Blood*, Chapter 7.

5. Bateson, Gregory. *Style, Grace, and Information in Primitive Art*, Wenner-Gren Conference on Primitive Art, 1976.

6. Armstrong, R.P. *Wellspring: On the Myth and Source of Culture*, pg.19.

7. Stephen, Alexander. *Hopi Journal of Alexander Stephen*, Columbia University Press, quoted in Polly Schaafsma's *Kachinas in the Pueblo World*, Chapter 4.

8. Hieb, Louis. "*The Meaning of Katsina: Toward a Cultural Definition of 'Person' in Hopi Religion*," quoted in Polly Schaafsma's *Kachinas in the Pueblo World*, Chapter 4.

9. Lockwood, Sandra. *Thin Places*. Master of Arts in Liberal Studies. Simon Fraser University. Spring 2013.

10. Crawford, Mathew. 'the world shows up' is a frequent expression in *The World Beyond Your Head.*

11. Bateson, Gregory. *Style, Grace, and Information in Primitive Art*, Wenner-Gren Conference on Primitive Art, 1976.

BIBLIOGRAPHY

Armstrong, Robert Plant. *Affecting Presence: An Essay on Humanistic Anthropology,* University of Illinois Press. 1986.

Armstrong, Robert Plant. *Wellspring: on Myth and Source of Culture,* University of California Press, 1975.

Basso, Keith. *Wisdom Sits in Places: Landscape and Language Among the Western Apache,* University of New Mexico Press, 1996.

Bateson, Gregory. *Steps to an Ecology of Mind,* Ballantine Books, 1972.

Childs, Craig. *House of Rain: Tracking a Vanished Civilization across the American Southwest,* Back Bay Books, 2006.

Crawford, Matthew. *The World Beyond Your Head: Becoming an Individual in the Age of Distraction,* Farrar, Straus and Giroux, 2016.

Dewitt, John McKee. "The Unrelenting Land," in *The Spell of New Mexico,* editor Tony Hillerman, University of New Mexico Press, 1984.

De Zengotita, Thomas. *Mediated: How the Media Shapes Your World and The Way You Live in It.* Bloomsbury, 2005.

Lillard, Charles. *Just East of Sundown: The Queen Charlotte Islands,* Horsdal & Schubart, 1995.

Lockwood, Sandra. *Thin Places,* Simon Fraser University Master's Thesis, 2013.

Norberg-Schulz, Christian. *Genius Loci: A Phenomenology of Architecture,* New York, Rizzoli, 1980.

Quillien, Jenny. "*Here: Mankind as Counterpoint*", *Tell it Slant*, Volume XVII, Santa Fe Home Press, December June 2011.

Quillien, Jenny. "*Haunted Spaces for Lesser Gods: a more modest interpretation of Christopher Alexander's findings in Book Four of The Nature of Order,*" International Association of Environmental Philosophy, Washington, D.C. June 2010.

Schaafsma, Polly (editor), *Kachinas in the Pueblo World*, University of New Mexico Press, 1994.

Scott, James. *Seeing Like a State*, Yale University Press, 1999.

Semple, Ellen Churchill. *Influences of Geographic Environment: On the Basis of Raztel's Anthropo-Geography*, New York: Henry Holt & Co., 1911.

Stuart, David, E. *Anasazi America*, University of New Mexico Press, 2014.

Theroux, Paul. *The Tao of Travel*, Houghton Mifflin, Boston, 2012.

Turner, Victor. *Blazing the Trail: Way Marks in the Exploration of Symbols*, University of Arizona Press, 1992.

Vaillant, John. *The Golden Spruce: a True Story of Myth, Madness, and Greed*, Vintage Canada, 2005.

Weigle, Marta. *Brothers of Light Brothers of Blood: The Penitentes of the Southwest*, University of New Mexico Press, 1976.

Whyte, David. *Crossing the Unknown Sea: Work as a Pilgrimage of Identity*, Penguin Putnam, 2001.

PHOTO CREDITS

Front cover. Paintings by Peter Nisbet, with permission

Burial tree. Tana Toraja, Sulawesi, Indonesia. Photo Charles Adams

Old growth forest. Photo Charles Adams

Drawing of old forest from drawingthemotmot.com

Drawing from Four Corners from sketchplease.com

Cedar Mesa. Photo Peter Nisbet with permission

Mesa Verde with tourists. Google images. com

Unvisited hideout. Photo Jenny Quillien

Hideout location. Photo Charles Adams

Abiquiu morada. Photo pininterest.com

Penitentes of Abiquiu. Photo pininterest.com

Transformation Mask. Collected on Haida Gwaii (probably at Skidegate) in 1879 by Israel W. Powell.CMC VII-B-20 (S86-386) Canadian Museum of History, Ottawa

Bricolage Mask. Pacific Coast Mask Collection. Royal British Columbia Museum, Victoria. Photo Charles Adams

Gagiid mask. Canadian Museum of History, Ottawa

Kwakiutl Fool Mask. Royal British Columbia Museum, Victoria. Photo Charles Adams

Alaskan mask. Canadian Museum of History, Ottawa

Mudhead kachina. Photo pininterest.com

Buffalo Dancer. Picuris Pueblo. Photo modified from David M.Kennedy

Mudhead drawing. Roediger, V.M., *Ceremonial Costumes of the Pueblo Indians*, University of California Press, 1941, page 231.

Mudhead dancers. Photo ioxoco-facade.blogspot.com

Disintegrating adobe. Photo Jenny Quillien

Parasynzki on Everest. Photo from Spaceref.com

Camping. Sketch from 123kindergarten.com

Wolf drawing by Chevy Crowley

AUTHORS

Jenny Quillien. French/American. Jenny splits working time between Europe and the USA. Degrees in anthropology (Licence, Paris), linguistics (Maitrise, Strasbourg) and industrial psychology (3ème cycle, Montpellier) and a late-life Masters in Eastern Classics from St John's College, Santa Fe. Home is Santa Fe, New Mexico, the launching pad for many wanderings and hikes into her backyard liminal lands.

Sandra Lockwood. Canadian. BA (University of Toronto, Asian Studies); BFA (Emily Carr University); MALS (Simon Fraser University, Vancouver); PhD in progress (Simon Fraser University). Home is Vancouver and a Gulf Island cabin getaway.

ACKNOWLEDGEMENTS

The authors would like to thank their partners. Charles Adams for driving impossible non roads, photographing, and, as always, putting the first critical editorial eye on a draft. Mark Jowett for supporting esoteric endeavors and figuring out, long distance, how island power outages could screw up pumps, water tanks, and toilets that refuse to flush. They're good sports.

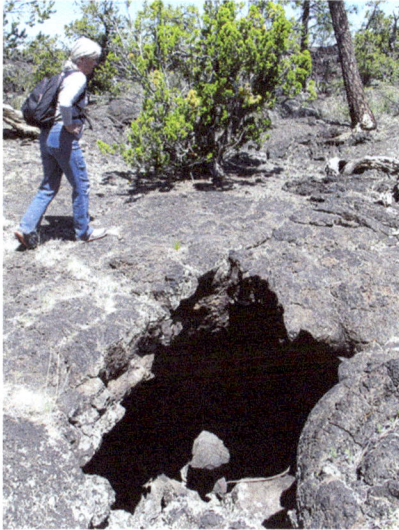

J. Quillien skirting cave-ins
on the lava flows in El Malpais of
New Mexico

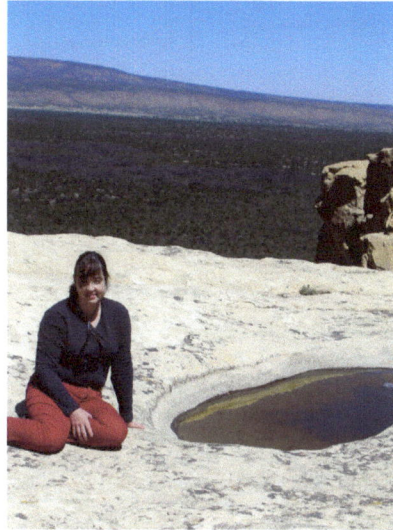

S. Lockwood inspecting tiny
crawfish which remain dormant in
dry mud but revive with rainwater

www.ingramcontent.com/pod-product-compliance
Lightning Source LLC
Chambersburg PA
CBHW060820270326
41930CB00003B/101